AS MOTHER
WOULD SAY...

.

As Mother Would Say...

by Mildred Taylor

Warmtree Press
2013

Warmtree Press
232 Red Arrow Road
Ligonier, PA 15658

FIRST EDITION

ISBN: 978-0-9888154-0-7

Page 128: Photo Credit: Courtesy of NASA

These words are dedicated to Amelia Freda Endt Pearson with thanks for giving me the words of a period of time that is gone, but not forgotten.

ACKNOWLEDGEMENTS

First I want to thank Gloria Price for suggesting my long list of Mother's sayings be put in specific episodic form. I thank Fred Peterson for guiding me to Todd Sanders who also gets a big round of applause for his help. Rosemary Coffee was wonderful in her thorough editing. Thank you, Rosemary. Sean Camp, a gifted photographer, gets many thanks for my picture session in St. Marys, Ontario, Canada. But most of all I feel both much gratitude and love for my husband, Gus, for putting the whole manuscript in order as well as approving and proofing the late additions. Without Gus there would be no book.

FOREWORD

Mildred Taylor is an accomplished and award winning poet, having won Senior Poet Laureate for the state of Pennsylvania two years in a row; 2011 and 2012. She is a member of the Pennsylvania Poetry Society and is a member and past president of the Pittsburgh Poetry Society. She has been interested in poetry and writing from a very early age.

As a teacher for over 30 years she incorporated her love of Shakespeare into her classroom teaching. She used her literary talent to write short plays for younger children to learn and stage.

This book is an interesting and unique memoir of growing up in North Carolina in the 1930's and 40's, from a young child to going off to college. She uses an eclectic mix of prose and poetry which punctuates the narrative with the moving emotions of her poems. It is a poignant personal story of a time in our history that most people have forgotten or never learned.

E. GUSTAV TAYLOR......friend, fan, cheerleader
and admiring husband

PROLOGUE

Her name was Amelia Freda Endt. She was born December 4, 1906, in Ocean Springs, Mississippi. One of seven children, she was the youngest daughter, the next to youngest child. Her mother died when she was 7, and she, along with two other sisters, was raised by her mother's sister. Amelia remembered her Aunt Augusta as a large woman who ruled the household with steel fingers. She had six children of her own, and three more girls didn't help the household any. The only things Amelia ever mentioned about Uncle Albert were that he worked in a bar, smoked cigars, and sometimes made the children laugh by imitating people they knew. Aunt Augusta meted out food and discipline briefly and with iron certainty.

After graduating from high school, Amelia and her sister Leona went to Mobile, Alabama, to take a training course for telephone operators for the Bell Telephone Company. The girls – Amelia was 18, Leona 20 – had heard how big and busy Mobile was. Leona had seen an ad in the *Biloxi Times* by the Bell Telephone Company stating a need for efficient operators. The girls saved up some of their wages from their Saturday jobs at Woolworth and went by bus. Mobile was less than one hundred miles from Ocean Springs, so it seemed the practical thing to do. They could come back to Ocean Springs easily enough.

The girls rented a room in a boarding house run by Lydia Kuntz, who had been married to Emitt Kuntz for only two years. This was Lydia's second marriage, although she never spoke about her first husband.

Lydia had lived in Norfolk, Virginia, for years and liked it a lot, because it had a shipyard; even though the war was over, it was a thriving place and Lydia had worked there part-time. The girls finally wormed out of Lydia that Mr. Kuntz was in a concentration camp, though Lydia didn't say where, because he had sent messages on his shortwave radio to German submarines in the Gulf of Mexico. The girls figured Mr. Kuntz must have been from Germany, but Lydia never actually said.

The girls found out that Lydia had abandoned her first husband and four children when she hopped on the train in Norfolk, Virginia, with Mr. Kuntz, and went to Mobile. She never said why about that either.

Lydia's long-abandoned son, John Ashton Pearson, came seeking his mother in the spring of 1926, after the girls had been there a little over a year. John's father had died when John was eight, and his father's sister made all of the Pearson children, of which there were three boys and one girl, quit school and gain employment. John, being the youngest, found a job with a roofer and learned the trade. John had done little besides work for the Hanson Roofing Company in Norfolk, Virginia, until he was 20. He longed to find his real mother, as his Aunt Ethel often told him that he and his two brothers and sister didn't make enough money to merit eating off of her. John, who was very thrifty, scouted around to find out what he could about his mother. He got the final information he needed from the Norfolk Shipyard, where Lydia had worked part-time. A worker told him she went to Alabama, to a city that started with M, and that she went with a Mr. Kuntz, a German fellow, "very smart." The two of them were often seen together in bars. Those were her young days, and Lydia was a looker.

John met Amelia at Lydia Kuntz's boarding house. After a brief courtship, John and Amelia married in 1927. They moved back to Norfolk, Virginia, where John had a job as an automobile mechanic.

The Great Depression of 1929 was very hard on the Pearsons. During these lean years, Amelia saved every possible penny. The couple and their infant daughter finally moved to Elizabeth City, North Carolina, in 1933, where John got a better job in an automobile repair shop.

Amelia lived in Elizabeth City for the next 48 years. John died in 1969. Her two daughters married and moved away. Eventually, she herself moved to Grand Junction, Colorado, to be near her younger daughter. She spent the last eight years of her life missing Elizabeth City. Amelia died in 2000 at the age of 94.

14

Amelia Pearson loved her home and kept it impeccably neat. She kept herself just as neat. Her main love was gardening; when she finally had her own home in her late forties, she made her yard a showplace. People came from as far away as Norfolk to see the large spray of azaleas across the back of her yard. Daisies, larkspur, snapdragons, bachelor buttons, and many other colorful flowers surrounded the house. People said she had ten green fingers, and all ten were marked with soil. It was amazing how each year she saved seeds from her plants - indeed, she never bought seeds, not even tomato. Her azaleas were started from cuttings placed in a tin can of water sitting on her window sill in the kitchen.

Her communication with her daughters, Cece and Ann, was mostly non-existent. She passed her knowledge and ethics down to them with adages, also known as platitudes, maxims, or wise sayings. When either child asked a question, her answer was an adage or a brief remark. This puzzled Cece for years, but she learned to accept the fact that she had to read a book or ask the mother of one of her friends for answers to questions about, say, sex or college. In a very strong way, this made Cece independent. She learned to find out things on her own. But it also made Cece feel alienated from Amelia and lonely in a strange way. Cece also thought Amelia was beautiful and tall, although she later found out that Amelia was only 5'1". Her black hair and pale blue eyes were the opposite of Cece, who had corn-silk hair and dark blue eyes.

Amelia never came to a parent conference with Cece's teachers. She never was homeroom mother for holidays, though Cece begged her to provide cookies just one time. Even when Cece made the Honor Society for academic achievement, Amelia wouldn't come to the initiation ceremony. All Cece ever got was a saying that was supposed to suffice. This book will tell some of those almost forgotten yet interesting sayings, most of which are now lost in cyberspace, replaced by meaningful conversations between children and parents that Amelia never had or knew how to give. Cece has tried a good many of these sayings on her younger grandsons, who recognize only a few, if any, of these clichés. They are precious to Cece because they represent Amelia and her insecurities, which Cece failed to understand as a child.

1

THREE SISTERS

It is more than a picture,
It is a special time that I didn't know.
Three young women in dropped waist dresses,
skirt just at the knees,
wearing cloche hats that cling
to their heads. Just a little bit of hair
juts out at the ears like feathers.
All three wear identical plain patent leather shoes
as well as thick looking stockings.
They stand on a pier with water in the background.

I know these women
with their wide-youth smiles.
I know a little of their world.
I know wars, poverty and hardships are their time.
I know each woman's singular future.
Two are my aunts. The water is the Gulf of Mexico.
The woman on the left and the one
in the middle will soon move to Mobile.
I know the middle woman's tomorrows
as I know my past as our times meet and become one.

2

CURIOSITY KILLED...

The Pearsons lived in Norfolk, Virginia, until their baby daughter, Cecelia, was almost three. John then decided that Norfolk was too big. Having heard about Elizabeth City, North Carolina, 48 miles southeast of Norfolk, he went scouting there and got a job in Anderson's Auto Shop. He rented an apartment on North Road Street, close to town and all the stores, the library, and the churches, because they had no car. There were no city busses. Amelia and Cece (Cecelia's nickname) moved into the five-room, first-floor apartment with only a crib and a bed.

Cece's first memory of North Road Street is Amelia telling John that she wanted a cedar chest, a Lane's cedar chest. John reminded her that it was 1935, and they had already been paying off a couch and easy chair. There would be no more furniture until later. Amelia said nothing. Instead, she started pinching pennies: less stew meat in the stew, chicken more often. Since John often let farmers pay off their debts to him with what they farmed, the Pearsons always had lots of potatoes, cabbage, and especially chickens. Many mornings Amelia would bring in a live chicken with its legs tied together as she picked up the morning paper. Although Cece avoided the chickens because she hated their bobbing heads and flapping wings, she loved the many chicken dishes Amelia cooked.

John was a good mechanic. More importantly, he was excellent with people. He was always smiling; he loved meeting new folks. Anderson, on the other hand, always came in late. John discovered that Anderson was a tippler. John soon realized that he was doing all the work, while

Anderson received half the profits. John visited the bank, got a loan of two hundred dollars, and bought the other half of the shop. This turned out to be a very smart move.

One morning in May, Amelia told Cece they were going to town. They walked to Parker's Furniture Store, where Amelia, always a slow decision-maker; put a beautiful Lane cedar chest on layaway. Cece had never heard of layaway before and thought that someday she would use it.

Several months later, the chest was delivered. Amelia called Cece into the bedroom and let her hold her head above the open chest and inhale.

Cece fell in love with the smell. Amelia closed the lid, and Cece knew this was Amelia's treasure chest. And so it was. Cece knew Amelia kept all sorts of things in that chest. It was locked and forbidden to Cece, but her curiosity kept gnawing at her. Cece thought of the gentle woody smell in the chest. She could catch a hint of the scent when Amelia opened it, while Cece stood in the hall outside the bedroom. It made Cece think of crisp autumn leaves and forests. Cece was six years old and could read pretty well. She knew Amelia saved special newspapers that told of events that interested her such as articles about Europe and a war. She had a feeling Amelia kept other special things in the chest, too, but she couldn't imagine what.

One day Amelia went next door to Mr. Cliff Sawyer's house to pay the rent. Cece snuck into the bedroom to look for the key to the cedar chest. She knew the key had to be in Amelia and John's bedroom. She quickly riffled though all of the drawers. No key. Cece was nervous, but she knew Amelia always talked to Martha and Mary, Mr. Sawyer's daughters, for a good while each month. Next Cece went through all of Amelia's shoe boxes and hat boxes, for Amelia was a keeper. No key. Finally, Cece gave up just a few minutes before Amelia came home. Cece sighed with relief; her get-away was clean.

Cece felt a little guilty at having rummaged through Amelia's things, but she was so curious. Maybe Amelia had silk scarves, fancy nightgowns, or even rubies and pearls in the chest. But Cece had a feeling of success just because she hadn't been caught.

Wrong. The next morning, when Cece walked into the kitchen, Cece knew she was "caught" when she saw Amelia's hands on her hips, her face grim. "Curiosity killed the cat," was all Amelia said. Cece didn't learn the rest of the saying for years; "satisfaction brought her back." Cece waited for more words as her heartbeat doubled. She felt cold all over, but Amelia said nothing more.

Cece's inquisitiveness often got her into trouble, especially in relation to prohibitions she disagreed with: thus she learned about fire by stealing matches and burning twigs, and often grabbed a couple of apples from the Sawyers' apple tree, which she knew was off limits, even though the Sawyers let them rot every year. Cece's tongue was her worst offender, but somehow she just had to say what came into her head in almost any given situation; especially when she was sassing Amelia, the words just sort of "fell" out of Cece's mouth before she could think to stop them. Cece really never learned to completely control her words, but she got more temperate as the years went on. This trait resulted in Amelia repeating more adages to her daughter. Amelia used her firmest voice when doing so. One of Amelia's favorites was, "You're a loose cannon!"

3

THE HOUSE WITH DIVIDENDS

We were the only tenants
on the block, (once THE block).
The bourbonded black sheep of the family next door
needed money for more.
Thus we were a crew of trawler-transients
amid a convoy of Sawyer luxury liners.

Our ship had its blemishes;
cracked plaster, a floor plan butchered
to a puzzle of apartment-conversion,
stuck windows, few screens, dull gray paint,
no central heat, and an entire back yard
isolated by a tired chicken-wire fence.

But most of these were dividends.
The plaster cracks were a chameleon-medley
of animals and flowers.
Unopened windows were transparent canvases
for finger drawing.
You could crawl through or perch on the windowsills

of the screenless windows
that didn't stick.
Coal sketches didn't show up clearly on gray paint.
You could warm socks, and underwear
on an oil heater in the living room,
but not on central heating.

Tall tiger lilies poked
between the hexagonal hoops of the fence.
Layers of honeysuckle entwined both fence and lilies
in an aura of yellow and white syrup.
The honeysuckle provided daily dextrose.
The lily stalks provided summer smoking.

And there was a fig tree w-a-y in the back yard.
Twice as tall as every house on the block,
this giant unfolded a hundred limbs,
spreading; fanning up to
a multifingered palm
of hairy leaves and fruit.

No task was too great to ask
of this tree.
It was smoking room, hiding place, snack bar,
observatory for sun, clouds, and stars;
laboratory of insects and seasons,
cove for reading, wondering, and healing.

My parents did not appreciate these extras
the house graciously gave.
But when we moved,
my Mother took a cutting from the fig tree
and planted it in her new back yard.
Every house needs dividends.

..............*Written circa 1954*

4
TRYING TIMES

It was a time of hopscotch, marbles, and jump rope.
Mothers cooked and cleaned. Fathers went to work.
Our radio shaped like a Gothic arch told of Germany
swallowing country after country.

It was a time of Wonder Bread for ten cents a loaf,
a milkman putting a pint of milk on the porch each morning,
when oleomargarine came with a packet of orange powder
you had to mix with a fork to turn it into "butter."

This was a time of each child having assigned chores,
doing homework without being told,
of saying "sir" and "ma'am" to adults,
and learning table manners they used all their lives.

This was a time of penny candy at the corner store,
Mary Janes, cinnamon squares, candy cigarettes,
when gum was five cents a pack that few kids could afford,
and pined for Teaberry, the latest flavor.

There were the Curies who discovered radium,
Einstein, a patent clerk, analyzing light and speed,
Salk beating the polio plague,
Oppenheimer, Fermi, the Manhattan Project.

The world raged: War Bonds, Uncle Sam wants you,
"A slip of the lip might sink a ship," as Japan
spat fire like a rampant dragon.
There were rationing, shortages, blackouts.

It was a time when a gold band on the left hand
married you forever to one person,
when women dropped their maiden names.
and few children knew the word divorce.

There was the Berlin Airlift
for a fiercely fractured Germany,
as Stalin plotted to absorb
Balkan countries into Communism.

The world was bleeding, and it was not
the blood to end all wars.
It was a time of healing, a footing
with intense expectations and deep concern.

5

IT'S AN ILL WIND...

One night Amelia was working on the books for the shop. She couldn't understand John's poor handwriting on one bill, so she called the Elks Club and asked for him. She was told John wasn't there. When questioned, the gentleman on the line told Amelia that John had not been in that evening at all.

When John came home, Cece was in bed, but not asleep. Her heart was beating so fast. She heard Amelia ask John where he had been. He said "The Elks Club, of course." After that, Cece turned on her side, clutched a pillow, and put the other pillow over her head so she couldn't hear what was being said.

All Cece could think about was John's first girlfriend. Cece had been six and going into first grade in a few weeks. Her name was Lila, and Cece didn't know how Amelia found out about her, but Amelia and Cece were on the train to Ocean Springs, Mississippi, within two days. Cece remembered Amelia crying softly. She remembered the musty train and trying to think of what to say to Amelia. If Cece asked what state they were in, Amelia just looked away. It was a long two-day ride, but Cece didn't cry. Somehow she felt dry inside.

Cece entered first grade in Ocean Springs. Amelia visited her four sisters, who still lived there. Theresa, Ethel, Maude, and Leona offered room and board to Amelia and Cece.

Amelia alternated a week with each one, while Cece insisted on staying with her favorite, Aunt Theresa. Aunt Theresa was fun. She was short

and fat and had beautiful curly red hair that she let Cece brush each day, as she washed her hair daily. Aunt Theresa did mention to Cece that she dyed her hair herself. Cece wondered how she did it. Aunt Theresa scrubbed the floors of her whole house daily as well. All the floors were linoleum, and Aunt Theresa let Cece run and slosh all through the house as she threw buckets of water across the floors. Aunt Theresa drank two or three beers a day and let Cece take a small sip every once in a while. Aunt Theresa read romance novels and told Cece some of the plots. Cece was having fun for the first time that she could remember.

September came and Cece entered first grade. She trotted off to school sparkling clean from Aunt Theresa's bathtub, knowing she smelled of Lux. She felt bouncy and happy. She seldom saw Amelia, for she was busy telling each family member about her heartbreak. Aunt Theresa kept Cece so occupied that she hardly thought of John, though every now and then she wondered what Lila looked like and why John liked her better than Amelia and Cece.

Near the end of October, John showed up. Cece sat in the swing with Aunt Theresa on her back porch, straining to hear the mumbling in the kitchen between Amelia and John. Aunt Theresa hummed "Kentucky Babe" to relax, but it only made hearing anything harder.

Three days later the three Pearsons were on a train headed to Norfolk, Virginia, where they caught a bus to Elizabeth City. Cece was upset and very nervous. She hated making new friends all over again. She liked Miss Bell, her teacher in Ocean Springs. When Cece started to say something about her feelings, Amelia said, "Blood is thicker than water." Cece felt like crying, but she bit her bottom lip instead. Cece remembered her feelings forever.

In a few years it happened again. On this occasion, Cece tossed back and forth all night, and sure enough, next morning, Cece found Amelia sitting at the kitchen table with her hands over her face, quietly weeping. This time it was in Springfield, Massachusetts, at Aunt Dorothy's house, where they landed. Aunt Dorothy and her two children lived in a three-story house on Spring Street. Aunt Dorothy's husband was Amelia's older brother Henry, who had died at fifty-two of a heart attack.

The children slept on the third floor, which was cold, but not as cold in February as it was outside. Ann was now four and slept in the bedroom with Amelia. Cece had never seen snow before, and her love for it lasted about three days. On the third day, which was a Monday, the three children walked six blocks to school. Jackie was in tenth grade. She was quiet and studious and ignored Cece, who was in sixth grade and taller than Jackie, which surprised her. Cece was about normal at five feet. She was secretly jealous of Jackie's long brown hair that the older girl let fly free in the bitter cold wind. Allen, Aunt Dorothy's son, was in fourth grade; he was funny, always telling school stories, especially about how mean the nuns were. He pulled Cece's short yellow hair and called her a slow southerner, which Cece didn't understand.

Allen was so right. Most of the nuns were ferocious, especially Sister Josepha Mary. She was very tall and thin, pinched her lips together all day long, and carried a ruler in her right hand. All day she tapped the ruler on her left hand as if practicing for attack. And attack she did. If you held your pencil wrong, she would whack across the top of your hand with her weapon. In Elizabeth City, you could hold a pencil any way that was comfortable. Here you lost ten points if you didn't dot an "i" or forgot a period. Cece, who had always loved school and had done very well, became a nervous wreck. Her stomach clenched itself, and she couldn't eat. To top it all, Cece had Sister Josepha Mary for every class but math. She had Sister Miriam Joseph for math, and for the first time ever Cece actually liked math class. Sister Miriam Joseph moved around the classroom constantly. She always had a smile on her face. She tousled Cece's hair once, when Cece scored one hundred percent on a test. Cece loved her

But Cece had Sister Josepha Mary practically all day. The day started with the Pledge of Allegiance to the flag, the Lord's Prayer, and three Hail Marys. Cece never understood why Mary got three prayers and God only one. Everyone stood for that ritual. After that no one could sit down at their desk until they shared something helpful they had done before coming to school. It could not be the same thing every day. Cece went through making her bed, getting in the newspaper, and bringing in the milk. Then she was stumped. That was all that Amelia and Aunt Dorothy required of her. Amelia had told Cece what a terrible thing it is to lie, stressing that God watched every move and heard every word everyone said.

The night before the fourth day in Sister Josepha Mary's class, Cece was awake most of the night. She thought and thought, making up things that she could have done to help around the house. The next day, Cece made a big decision: she lied. She said she dried the dinner dishes, which was Allen's job. From then on Cece got even more creative. She even shoveled snow, which Aunt Dorothy hired some gentleman to do, because Aunt Dorothy was a widow. Because of these inventions, Cece never had to stand up all day in Sister Josepha Mary's class.

It was so cold. Elizabeth City was never as cold as Springfield. By the time Cece and Jackie walked the six blocks, their knees as well as their noses were fire-truck red. Allen had on long pants, so he was almost all right, but Cece's coat had been bought in Elizabeth City, and wasn't thick and warm like Jackie's and Allen's coats. Cece began to hate everything about Springfield and wished John would show up.

John did arrive in the middle of March. Cece, Jackie, and Allen stayed upstairs on the third floor, but they could catch some of the screaming. Aunt Dorothy, who was the loudest, called John names Cece knew were terrible but had never heard before. The battle lasted for days. Cece lost count. Finally, Amelia told Cece to pack, and the Pearsons headed south. Cece was thrilled. She would finish the school year with her old friends. It was a rather silent trip back. For the first time, John asked all about Cece's school. When Cece told about Sister Josepha Mary's ruler, Amelia said that the nun probably just tapped the children's hands. Cece started to comment, but she had finally learned that it didn't pay to correct Amelia. After all, blood was thicker than a lot of liquids. And when Amelia told Cece they were going home, she said that forgiveness is the greatest virtue a person can have, and that she is a forgiving person. Cece remembered hearing that somewhere. But Cece thought of one of Amelia's sayings when things were bad; "It's an ill wind that blows no good," which Cece felt was really true this time. She was going home to warmth and to her friends.

6
NIGHT WALK

Momma holds my hand real tight,
leading, almost pulling me
away from 310 North Road Street,
trudging up one street,
down another, then another,
and another
until she spots Daddy's tow truck.

Momma stops, stands still as ice,
her eyes darting back and forth
from Daddy's truck to
the white wooden house
with the upstairs windows
gleaming like pale yellow eyes
dimmed by the lids of window shades.

I glance up at Momma
staring at the windows.
I look around and
suddenly
Momma grabs my arm,
turns, almost runs,
pulling me,
my heart pounding
faster and faster
shortening my breath more and more,
and somehow I know something
I do not know how to say.

Daddy,
why didn't you explain something,
anything
to help me understand
why we went to the Alkrama
every Saturday and watched
Roy Rogers or Gene Autry
in a black and white west
twice?

You never said a word
as we walked five blocks there,
sat for three hours,
walked five blocks back
into the bristling room.
There we were

the three of us
in the kitchen
as the trap snapped shut.
The riddle of her fury
bitter as bile,
erupted.
She threw a dish
across the room.
You never said a word.
You left me standing there
to run to my room.

8

AUNT THERESA'S FLOCK

Aunt Theresa muttered about the cost of crab meat,
The Englishman taking every cent, even the car,
The oldest son playing hooky from school.
as she eyed the sky for sunrise.

Aunt Theresa married an Englishman when she was fifteen,
divorced him at twenty one because all he did was smoke cigars,
play poker and drink bourbon.
Aunt Theresa then dyed her hair henna
and raised three sons from the take out restaurant she made in her garage.

Always tired, angry at the world and God,
Aunt Theresa put her Virgin Mary in the garbage can,
tossed her rosary in the Gulf of Mexico, and bought twenty chickens.
Each morning after the sun was full up, she strolled out to the chicken yard
scattered grain as waves of wings fluttered toward her
heads bobbing up and down like corks.

Aunt Theresa muttered about the cost of crab meat, the Englishman
   taking every
cent, even the car, the oldest son playing hooky from school.
She looked down at her flock that demanded nothing but grain, water and
an occasional raking of the yard while giving daily eggs, flesh and comfort.

Her oldest son ended up on a riverboat on the Mississippi,
doing what his father did.
The second learned Aunt Theresa's gumbo recipe, the mixture for her
famous stuffed crabs and the secret ingredient in her pecan pie.
The last boy taught math right there in Ocean Springs High School.

The younger boys finally forced Aunt Theresa to stop cooking.
She then read romance novels, scrubbed the back porch more often
and several times each day waded among her chickens
smiling, feeling avenged.

9

CHILDREN SHOULD BE SEEN...

Cece saw doing the weekly grocery shopping with Amelia as a tedious, dull chore, but Amelia insisted that Cece accompany her. To Amelia, it was a social event, a chance to meet friends, make new ones, and simply chat her way through the store. It was one l-o-n-g ordeal for Cece. Since Amelia knew every clerk in every department, even the stock people talked with her while on their knees loading cans of beans onto the shelves. Not only did Amelia chat with old friends, church friends, Cece's teachers (although sharing nothing about Cece), and bingo club friends, but she made new acquaintances each week who quickly became friends. Strangers were anyone who happened to pause beside Amelia to squeeze a lemon or prod a head of lettuce. They were immediately drawn into a conversation. Amelia was involved in what we now call networking. It drove Cece nuts.

Amelia always discussed world news with the butcher, while Cece steamed the glass meat case with her breath and wrote "hurry" or "boring" in the steam. Cece often wished that Amelia would talk with Cece like that about school or even a bit of the world news Cece gathered once in a while. It was 1941, and Europe was in a war, which Amelia and the butcher seemed to know a lot about. Every now and then Cece would pull Amelia's sleeve and murmur about leaving. All she ever got from Amelia was a glare like machine-gun fire and another saying, "Children should be seen and not heard." Or "Silence is golden." Cece had begun writing down some of Amelia's clichés to use on someone at school – not a teacher, of course, but someone who was teasing her about her straight hair or her skinny legs. However, most of Amelia's quips just didn't apply to Cece's school life.

School was Cece's refuge. She was in sixth grade now, what they called Junior High. She loved every class, even Civics, though Mrs. Klingensmith was scary because she was so big, had a big deep voice, and never smiled. Learning about the government was interesting, and when they had to memorize Lincoln's Gettysburg Address as well as the Preamble to the Constitution, Cece enjoyed learning such important things by heart. She wished Amelia would let her recite them to her. Then, one day, when Cece started to say; "Fourscore and seven years ago our forefathers set forth upon this continent…," Amelia interrupted, saying that she wondered when they would teach the children something useful in that school.

10

A STILL TONGUE...

Cece got into trouble often at school due to her tongue. She always sat in the back row in class so she could chat softly to the people around her. Inevitably she was moved to the front row in every class.

This slowed her whispering down. She wrote notes. She mouthed short sentences. She always got caught. She would lose recess or write an essay on a topic the teacher gave her.

One day Cece not only lost recess, wrote an essay on school manners, she had to "sit in" for an hour after school. Amelia got a phone call from Miss Winson, Cece's fourth grade teacher.

When Cece finally got home from school, Amelia said, "A still tongue has a wise head". Cece felt stupid. She resolved to try harder to zip her lips during class.

11
MANY HANDS...

One of Cece's jobs was helping Amelia prepare dinner. Cece was the chopper of anything that required chopping. She was also in charge of anything that needed to be grated.

One afternoon, Amelia was making vegetable soup, which involved a lot of chopping. There were tomatoes to peel and chop. Carrots, potatoes, celery, and onions were on the list as well. Amelia put the water on the oil stove, watched it come to a boil, dropped in the beef bone, and went to take her usual afternoon nap, which meant a two-hour rest. Cece was avidly chopping carrots into chunks. As Amelia left, she said, "Many hands make light work." Cece had often heard this and wished she had more hands every time.

It was years later when Cece was glad she had been sous chef to Amelia. When she got married, Cece already knew how to cook several basic meals.

12
A GERMAN WORD

Being of 100% German heritage, Amelia knew one or two German words. The only one Cece really learned because of its frequent use was arsch. It seemed to satisfy any inner rage Amelia felt in almost every situation. She mixed arsch with English adages elegantly.

"He gives me a pain in my arsch."

"Don't look up a dead horse's arsch."

"He/she doesn't know his/her arsch from third base." (This was often used when driving)

"Kiss my arsch." (Watch out, she was really angry.)

Cece used Amelia's "She doesn't know her arsch from third base" in Girl Scouts when her bridge partner made a dumb play. The leader promptly gave her a lecture on profanity as well as incorrect English.

13

THINGS MY FATHER TAUGHT ME

My father's arm slides across the kitchen table.
He glimpses at me as his grease-mapped hand
smacks, turns, flips snaps cards
until I nod I understand
this new solitaire.

Each night my father and I listen to
Hitler's words
hitting the air like huge fists,
my father frowning as he points out Germany,
Austria Czechoslovakia, Hungry, Poland, Netherlands, Belgium,
Luxembourg, France on a map,
explains *blitzkrieg, annexation, tyrant,*
muttering about weak hearts.

I ride beside my father in his tow truck
bouncing toward Norfolk
for parts to fix a wreck in the shop.
He points to the Dismal Swamp
sweeping by us in a spooky blur,
says George Washington helped survey it,
pounds the dashboard
the second we leave North Carolina,
smiling as he asks if the air smells different in Virginia.

We pile car parts in the back of the truck,
my father promising Mr. Pender
he will paint the Pender Paint and Parts truck as payment
like lots of farmers pay him
with chickens, cabbage, potatoes
for service on their farm equipment.

From my bedroom window
I watch the truck as my father
disappears into a long night
of poker and bourbon at the Elks Club,
and I am caged
in my mother's bitterness
trying to decide if barter
means more than money
like my father said.

14

ONE FOR THE ROAD

Wesley Saunders owned the Carolina Lumber Company. It was a family business; had been for generations. Wesley "ran" the company, which meant he dropped by several times weekly. Mostly Wesley dropped by to flirt with the secretaries.

Wesley hit the beach often, both in summer and winter. There was always action at Nags Head. One night coming from the beach rather late after having "one for the road," Wesley side swiped a tree. Wesley was not hurt, but his Oldsmobile was smashed all along the right side. Wesley cursed, and thought of Auto Body and Fender Works.

John wrote up an estimate for repairs. Amelia, as always, checked it over and doubled it. Wesley told John the estimate was a fair price, but he really wanted a new Ford. John offered Wesley a price for the smashed Olds. Wesley, who couldn't have cared less as he was tired of the four year old Olds, agreed.

John set to work fixing the Olds. The motor was in good condition. Tires were perfect. Once the body work was done, the car looked as good as new. John had trouble finding the right shade of red to match the car at Elizabeth City Paint & Supply Co., so he and Cece drove to the Norfolk Paint Company to match the color. Cece took a scraping from the Olds herself.

No luck in Norfolk. Cece began looking at the paint cans lined up on the long shelf in the paint company. A soft green caught her eye. She took the can to John. John nodded. Cece knew she had picked the perfect color. Cece also knew the car was to be a big surprise for Amelia. She bit her lip not to let the "cat out of the bag" as John had told her.

The 1938 Oldsmobile was finally finished. John had painted the top a lighter green than the bottom. When John drove it home instead of the beat up tow truck, both Amelia and Cece gasped. It was beautiful. It was1942, and the car looked like a car of the future. Amelia had to sit on a front step to catch her breath. Cece couldn't wait to tell everyone at school. John said; "I'm glad Wesley had one for the road." Amelia smiled and said; "And now WE have one for the road." Amelia and John had been married sixteen years.

15

STEPPING IN TIME

Make the leap,
catch the beat, see the sweep,
down, up, over, down,
keep the rhythm, meet the rope-slap sounds.

Jump the exact moment
to the half-sung jingle;
meter of movement,
metronome of rhyme,

"Last night and the night before
a lemon and a pickle came a-knockin' at my door.
I went downstairs to let them in,
and this is what they said to me,

    'Ladybug, ladybug, turn all around, around, around,
    ladybug, ladybug, touch the ground, ground, ground.
    Ladybug, ladybug, tie your shoe, shoe, shoe,
    ladybug, ladybug, how old are you, you, you?'"

Count the jumps, feel the breathy brush of space,
taste the clean, warm air
in the up and down joy
of a nine year old May morning.

16

BIRDS OF A FEATHER...

John had two brothers, Harry and Jake, both of whose families lived in Norfolk, Virginia, 48 miles from Elizabeth City. One day Uncle Harry called and invited the family to Norfolk for Sunday lunch. Uncle Jake and his wife Mary were coming, too. Cece was thrilled, though Amelia seemed a bit reluctant to go.

Off they went after nine o'clock Mass, arriving early at the home of Uncle Harry and his wife Lina. Uncle Harry and Aunt Lina had four children, three boys and a girl. Uncle Harry had a roofing business, which John related to because he had worked as a roofer as a child. Uncle Jake had red hair, which amazed Cece, because all the Pearsons had blond hair. Uncle Jake owned a bar called Pour More and bragged about his booming business. John thought that was a great name. It was a surprise to the three Pearson men that they all had businesses of their own and not one of them had come anywhere near finishing high school.

Uncle Harry's girl, Jean, was exactly Cece's age and very mature and spiffy. She had on slacks and a white blouse with wide cuffs that made her look grown up. She had pierced ears with small bead-like earrings. She was taller than Cece, had very straight teeth, which Cece did not, and boasted naturally curly brown hair. She was friendly and loved paper dolls, too.

Cece had brought her Shirley Temple paper dolls and was thrilled that Jean had a set, too. It was swell. They pretended the paper dolls were twins, and Cece loved every minute of pretending. Ann watched quietly for a while, then went to ride a tricycle that belonged to one of the boy cousins.

After lunch Cece and Jean went on with the paper doll fun while the adults sat around the big round wooden kitchen table and talked, laughed loudly and drank beer, except for Amelia who chose Dr. Pepper. Cece never saw Amelia drink any alcohol, though John had a bourbon and water every evening before dinner. The girls paid little attention to the laughter or jokes. Once Jean put her hands over her ears and rolled her eyes. Cece laughed.

The afternoon flew by, and soon it was time to drive back to Elizabeth City. They were on the road barely five minutes when Amelia said, "Birds of a feather flock together, and we are definitely not of that feather. Drinking beer all afternoon, and those jokes were awful."

Cece wondered if John felt the same as Amelia. He had a beer or two and he laughed a lot at the jokes. John shook his head, while Cece remembered the long, dull Sunday afternoon rides Amelia demanded each week as they passed old houses, new houses, partially built houses, and even back roads through the city. She knew Shirley Temple would never have a twin sister again. Cece felt hurt because she had family so close. Amelia refused to invite them back. John said nothing, but started going to the Elks Club every night.

17

B-I-N-G-O

Amelia belonged to a club appropriately named The Bingo Club. The membership was limited to eleven ladies, who took turns hosting the group, leaving January vacant because it was cold and the heat would have to be turned up if they met then. The ladies chipped in equally to purchase a fine bingo set. The ladies were all thrifty, though Amelia was known to be still in Depression mode. The monthly hostess was the caller.

Amelia seldom "BINGOED," but she didn't mind because she said her luck was her health. In December each year the ladies drew a slip of paper that designated the month they would be hostess the next year. So once a year Amelia planned her event, focusing on the dessert served after twenty games of bingo. Amelia calculated to the penny how much each treat cost. One year, since John's shop was doing well and he seemed to have stopped spending money the wrong way, Amelia decided to splurge. Recollecting that raspberry Jell-O with canned fruit, brownies, apple cake, and bread pudding were all served often, Amelia told Cece she was going to make this bingo meeting special.

One of the biggest problems each hostess had was coming up with twenty prizes for the twenty games they always played. A bar of soap, a spool of thread, a small bottle of shampoo, a pot holder, a dish towel, a small memo pad were all acceptable. This time Amelia bought a thimble. Cece was impressed with Amelia's thinking of something unusual. Amelia had also bought herself a thimble, even though she herself did not sew; rather she had given Cece the task of sewing back on all buttons that came off the clothes of anyone in the family. Cece wore the thimble like a badge of honor.

The year Amelia had bingo club in April; her camellias were in full bloom. She was so proud of her camellia bushes as well as her whole yard, which was a picture of pinks, reds, and purples: a summer rainbow. As an extra touch of elegance, as each guest arrived, Amelia gave her a camellia bouquet enhanced with a tiny pink bow. She splurged on her dessert, too, planning to make her special fresh coconut cake. Cece watched Amelia crack open the coconut with a hammer. As they shared the coconut milk, Amelia told Cece that her job, as usual, was to grate the coconut. Cece was glad to do it, because she could sneak many chunks of fresh coconut into her mouth. Cece couldn't figure out why Amelia put so much extra into this meeting, until Amelia told her that John had gotten a contract to tend to the city buses, a new convenience for E. City.

The bingo event went as planned, and Amelia recounted the evening to John in her usual semi-critical way. Margie wore, as always, a very snug dress to show off her slender figure. Estelle asked for a second slice of cake, even though she had diabetes. And Louise had simply "let herself go"; she had put on so much weight! John said nothing, as he tried to read the paper. Cece had taken Ann, who was now five, to the drive-in with Walter Jay, her latest fellow. It was a double feature and Ann had, of course, fallen asleep. Cece knew Ann was too young for Humphrey Bogart or Ingrid Bergman.. When she got home, Amelia gave a full report on the party, but didn't ask Cece about how Ann behaved or about the movie. She did ask what Walter Jay's father did, and, as usual, Cece didn't know.

18

THE ORDER OF THINGS

Cece knew that Amelia was very well organized. Every knickknack was placed on her whatnot in the exact same spot after each dusting. Every towel was folded into three equal parts after being ironed. Cece followed the rigid rules as best she remembered, even when she ironed socks, towels, and sheets. She hated ironing sheets most of all, because they were so big and hard to handle. But she didn't mind helping Amelia, because she knew Amelia wanted the apartment and everything in it very clean.

One day Amelia told Cece to clean the walk-in pantry. It had five shelves, rather long ones, covered with miscellaneous foods. Cece immediately emptied all the shelves, placing all of the items outside the pantry on the kitchen floor. She scrubbed the shelves with soapy water, then rinsed them thoroughly. Next, she washed the floor and even wiped the pantry door inside and out. She then put the food back onto the shelves with a sigh of satisfaction.

A little while later Amelia yelled to Cece to come there at once. Amelia was standing inside the pantry. "You put everything in wrong; nothing is in the right order." Cece realized then that her sense of arrangement was very different from Amelia's. Amelia began taking the food off the shelves. She never changed, nor did Cece, in their sense of the order of things. Later, when every item was finally placed in the "correct" order, she turned to Cece and said, "You do things bassackward." Cece thought this was pig Latin, that funny game they played at school when the girls gossiped, thinking the boys wouldn't figure out what they were saying. When she thought about it, she realized Amelia was telling her she was unorganized and couldn't keep things straight. But Cece knew from her school grades that she did keep things straight when she wanted to, and that Amelia should have told her how to organize the groceries before she told Cece to do the cleaning.

19

WITHSTANDING: TO AMELIA

Slim and straight
she faced
being an orphan
caught in a cage of poverty,
left a dismal childhood
for a city and work,
successful with "Number, please,"
a sudden, swift marriage,
the Great Depression,
standing in line for a free soup bone,
never looking back,
step by step forward,
a long war, penny by penny,
Victory Gardens, rocky marriage,
forgiveness hidden beneath a veil of hurt,
children, hurricanes ridden out
in a closet with rosary in hand,
debt, thrift, sickness.
She stood slim and straight
shrouded in widowhood thirty four empty years,
held in silence,
withstanding.

20

GIVE YOU AN INCH...

By 1942 Amelia had the apartment fully equipped. The living room floor was covered with a maroon rug with big gold flowers. Cece thought it was the prettiest rug in the world. It reminded her of a fairyland. The mohair sofa and matching chair were paid for long ago, and Amelia had purchased two walnut end tables. They were round and she bought them during an after-Christmas sale. Amelia put one beside the sofa and the other beside the chair. John, who never cared what Amelia put in the house as far as furniture went, surprised Amelia one day and brought home two beautiful glass vases, one for each table. They were slender and tall and the color of the sky. Cece was afraid to touch them. Amelia warned her and John to keep a good distance between themselves and the vases. John laughed at these orders, because he never sat in the living room anyway. He was off to the Elks Club every night after supper. He played cards - poker, Cece found out later, and Cece was always asleep when John came home. Cece guessed that Amelia was asleep, too. Amelia liked to crochet and made afghans for her and John's bed and one for Cece's daybed that they opened at night and closed up during the day. Summer evenings she would work in her flower garden.

Cece loved dogs and often begged to go to the pound and get a puppy. Amelia wouldn't hear of it. Her apartment was spotlessly clean. Cece had trouble fitting her way of doing thing into such neatness. John was reasonably neat by nature, although Amelia's complaints about hair in the bathroom basin did no good.

John liked dogs, too. Amelia considered them vile, dirty things that messed up homes. One day John came home from work and mentioned that a stray mutt had been hanging around the shop for over a week. Of course, John had fed the poor creature and given him water. He had also given him a name: Spot. They were sitting at the supper table when John told them about Spot. Cece looked at Amelia. "Don't even think about it," Amelia said.

John took Cece to the shop the next Saturday to meet Spot. When they brought Spot home, John negotiated for Cece and Spot. Amelia finally relented. She said that Spot could stay in the yard and visit Cece on the back porch. Spot was all-white with big brown spots all over his body. His ears were really huge for his size, and Cece loved that. The yard was fenced in, and Cece quickly trained Spot not to go into Amelia's garden. Once in a while Cece would lift Spot into her bedroom through the back window, when Amelia and John were asleep. Unfortunately, Spot really needed a bath. Not only did Spot stink, he got dirt on the bed sheets.

Next food shopping day, Cece feigned a headache to get out of going along with Amelia. The moment Cece knew Amelia was gone, she started filling the bathtub, put Spot in the water, and began soaping and scrubbing. The water was still running when a scream pierced the happy scene: "What in God's name are you doing?" Cece immediately pulled the bathtub plug, grabbed a towel, and picked up Spot. Of course, Cece had to clean the bathroom; toilet included, plus wipe the walls around the bathtub with vinegar water to kill Spot's germs. Cece was glad the bathroom was small with white walls so she could see and remove every splatter. She even washed the mirror above the basin as well as the shelf below the medicine cabinet where John kept his shaving brush, soap, and razor. Cece felt certain Amelia would force John to take Spot to the pound, but she didn't. After the cleaning, the only punishment Cece got was that John grounded her for two weeks. This really didn't bother Cece, because she sat on the back porch reading Nancy Drew books with Spot sitting beside her. Amelia never said another word about the incident, but she constantly remarked on the infraction with adages:

"Give you an inch and you take a mile."

"You drive me up a wall."

"An apple doesn't fall far from the tree." (as she glanced back and forth from John to Cece)

"Sometimes I'm so mad, I could spit bullets."

"You mind your P's and Q's."

(Little did she know that this saying originally referred to pints and quarts of beer foaming too much!)

21

FRUGALITY, ECONOMY, GETTING AHEAD

Cece saw very little of John, because he worked such long hours and whiled away his free time at the Elks Club. He told Amelia this was good business, because he made contacts for work for the shop. Every morning Cece heard John get out of bed, go to the bathroom, and ready himself for work. He was fast and out of the house before six each morning. Amelia said John had a good reputation for doing excellent work, and he had just received a contract to paint all the school busses as well as fix any engine problems or dents. Cece knew that John made friends with everyone. He loved telling jokes that Cece didn't understand. Although he was short, Cece knew he was handsome. Amelia said he looked like a blond Clark Gable. When Cece saw "Gone with the Wind," she realized Amelia was right. Amelia was thrilled about their new prosperity, but kept her thrifty ways.

One day when John came home from work and sat on the bottom step in the mud room taking off his work shoes, he announced rather loudly that he had bought a lot at the end of Water Street. The Mellick Construction Company was to start building Pearson's Auto Body and Fender Works in two weeks. There would be no more rent to be paid on that dump he rented on Poindexter Street. The war had just ended, and the world was at peace at last. Amelia wiped her hands, sat down, and frowned. She gave a faint smile and said they could work it out. After all, things were going really well.

Amelia's sense of thrift went into overdrive. She doubled the size of the vegetable garden. Meat vanished from the family diet. The city was on the Pasquotank River, which not-too-distantly ended in the Atlantic Ocean about 38 miles away. Even though the price of seafood was reasonable, Amelia skipped Pender's Seafood Market; instead, three times weekly she and Cece met the fishermen very early in the morning as they were docking. Amelia got outstanding bargains on fish and crabs, as she was an expert negotiator. Cece got no new clothes. She wore hand-me-downs from her cousin in Baltimore, who was bigger than Cece. Few lights were allowed to burn unless absolutely essential. Amelia, John, and Cece learned very quickly to navigate in almost complete darkness. Cece's favorite and only treat, a thin slice of Milky Way once a day, was also eliminated.

John met each monthly mortgage payment promptly. Amelia smiled more often. Cece noticed that John had bought a new light brown serge suit with a vest and two pairs of pants. He topped it off with a straw hat with a brim all the way around it. Amelia observed that everyone should be thrifty with a $9,000 bank loan for the land and shop. John said nothing, as he left for the Elks Club. Cece sat on the back steps with Spot and did her homework. Spot leaned against her as he always did when he sensed Cece was nervous. Were Amelia and John in a thrift war?

22

THE LEDGER

Mother's head bends over a thick ledger;
the family *Domesday Book* of credits and debits.
Her arm rests on the checkerboard red and white tablecloth
as she carefully runs a pencil across the page;
circling here, striking out there.
Back and forth she goes
through the last months of our days.
Her head is covered in spit curls;
tight black spirals gripped by bobby pins.
Her face is furrowed to a frown,
her light blue eyes squinted.
The kitchen is quiet
as I tiptoe in from school.
I sit at the table beside her
while she balances our lives
with the trucks, cars and buses going in and out
of my father's shop.
I watch and wait,
hoping we will be able to have
pot roast on Sunday.

23

A NEW JOB

One night at supper John told Cece that he would give her a Saturday morning job if she wanted one. Her salary would 25 cents. All she had to do was clean his office and the bathroom in back of the shop. Cece was thrilled. That was a lot of money for an easy job.

After the first week Cece told John she would not clean the bathroom unless the toilet was flushed. John put up a big sign stating the necessity of flushing.

Cece loved the job. She got to mix with the crew. Bruce was an older man who said very little. Moses had worked for John the longest and the was very best at every job. Horse Boy was a farmer's son learning the trade from Moses. He worked too slowly to suit Moses, but his work was pretty good in sanding and taping a car for paint. Joey Jefferson was the newest member of the crew. He was in his early twenties. He had been in Chicago for two years. He said the wind blew him back to the south. Moses and JJ, as they called Joey, were black. That made no difference in the shop. It was work production that counted. Everyone mixed well but Bruce.

Cece loved talking to Moses and JJ. She knew there was such a thing as "colored town," but she thought it meant houses. JJ told her they had their own dime store, churches, grocery store and a theater that showed movies with all black casts. Cece didn't understand the reason for this because the stores on Main Street had plenty of stuff for everyone. The Carolina Theater was plenty big. It was like two cities. This seemed a waste. Then Cece remembered that there was a special all black school on the outskirts of town. Cece didn't know the word *integration*. She learned about it later. She did enjoy working around the shop and mixing with everyone but Bruce.

Amelia hadn't said much about Cece's new earnings. One night after dinner while Cece was drying the dinner dishes, Amelia said, "Always save for a rainy day." Cece knew this meant 'don't spend *any* of your money,' and Cece just hummed: "Over the Rainbow."

24
PAST RITUALS

Big, black, beautiful Moses Hinton
leans against the cinder block wall
of Auto Body and Fender Works.
Daddy stands beside him.
Both hold a cup of coffee.

Steam mists their faces as Daddy chuckles.
Mose, Moses nickname,
throws his head back and guffaws.
Each morning for many years
Mose gets to the shop just minutes after Daddy,

long before the rest of Daddy's crew. Mose and Daddy
roll up the shop doors, talk war news, make plans for the day's work.
Mose is the only man besides Daddy who can
clean radiators properly, pound a dented fender to silk,
paint a streakless car, never miss a day's work.

Saturday noon is payday and the shop closes.
Many Sunday mornings Lee Anderson calls Daddy.
Daddy goes to the jail, posts bail. Mose climbs into Daddy's tow truck,
Daddy starts the sputtering engine,
and they head silently toward Monday.

25

LITTLE AND OFTEN FILLS...

John had his first heart attack in his mid-forties. He was in the hospital for six weeks. Amelia virtually ran the shop, spending a lot of time there keeping tabs on everyone. She had been writing job estimates for John so long that she felt she was doing fine on the cost of new jobs. Cece did the best she could in the house to help Amelia, looking after Ann and keeping her grades up. Ann became Cece's shadow, following her everywhere. Amelia finally paid a neighbor to help Cece look after Ann because of Cece having to go on band trips. Cece was thrilled at her new hours of freedom and took advantage of them when she could. She would have a short date with Eddie, her current beau, or visit Nancy, one of her best friends, for an hour or so.

John sank deeper and deeper into depression, worrying over mortgage payments on the shop, which were to continue for four more years. When Amelia checked with the bank, she learned that they still owed $3,700. Amelia had that much and more in her cedar chest. She had been slipping dollars from John's wallet for a long time. His wallet was always stuffed then, and Amelia knew he gambled at the Elks Club, plus who knew what else?

Amelia hardly slept that night. Cece heard her moving through the apartment off and on until the wee hours. One morning, Amelia went to the bank, paid off the mortgage, and took the deed to Auto Body & Fender Works to John. This did the trick. John perked up and came home in a week. Cece never knew for sure where the money came from, but she suspected that Amelia's cedar chest was pretty well depleted. Cece finally gathered the courage to ask Amelia where she got the money. Amelia smiled and said, "Little and often fills a purse." Later that evening, she told Cece to remember that "Land is everything."

26

I'LL SWEAR

Amelia never used what we call "foul" language. She had her own words for venting. But when John had his first heart attack in his late forties, something precipitated her extreme anger. Amelia had always kept the books for Auto Body & Fender Works. She was impeccably precise with all the numbers, especially where the shop was concerned. John was in the hospital for a month, and Amelia was on overload; it was natural for her to assume that Bruce Williams, John's head mechanic, would look after things properly. After almost a month, John came home and returned to work, but only in the sense of sitting in the office. Amelia did the end-of-month books, checked back over the past six months, and quickly figured out that there had been a 20% decrease in profits. That evening she went over all the figures with John, who figured out what had happened. Bruce was evidently pocketing the money when a customer paid cash, which they often did when they had a radiator job done on their cars. It was one of the most lucrative areas of the business. Amelia gritted her teeth, slammed her fist on the table, and said, "That damn son of a bitch." John had a reputation of never facing up to a really bad situation, so Amelia went to the shop the next morning and fired Bruce. Cece had never heard such words from Amelia before and never heard them again.

27
...THE MICE WILL PLAY

When Amelia had her second daughter, Ann, it was 1944 and Cece was fourteen years old, plenty old enough for babysitting. This delighted Amelia, as it was free baby care. Cece was also delighted, for she had prayed for a baby sister or brother for a long time. Ann was a toy. Amelia never seemed to get around to bathing Ann, so Cece got to wash Ann every evening. She would soap Ann from head to toe and rinse her off with a sprinkle bottle Amelia used to dampen clothes before they were ironed. When Ann's hair needed to be washed, Cece would arrange Ann's shampoo-stiffened hair into weird arrangements: spikes all over her little head, a unicorn and one big curl in the middle. Cece loved it, and so did Ann. Amelia warned Cece about using too much soap and shampoo.

One evening Amelia and John went to a movie, leaving Cece to care for Ann, age 19 months and already walking. A delighted Cece at last had the opportunity to bounce Ann on the bed as high and as long as she liked, bathe her in a myriad of bubbles (strictly forbidden because it was a waste of soap), and mostly play hide and seek. Cece let Ann run and scream through the house as much as they both wanted. Unfortunately, Cece or Ann must have bumped into the end table in the living room, knocking over one of the blue vases John had given to Amelia. Hearing the crash, both girls froze. One of Amelia's precious vases was broken. Cece knew Amelia treasured these vases because they had been chosen by John. Plus, they were one of the first things Amelia had gotten for the apartment. Amelia always pointed them out when a friend visited for the first time.

Cece quickly cleaned up the broken glass and placed the other vase on the far back of the end table. It seemed to have grown during the accident, for now it looked like it was several feet tall. Cece placed folded newspapers in front of the monstrous thing, closing her eyes in dread.

When their parents came home, it took Amelia less than a second to spot the disaster area. With her hands on her hips, she cleared her throat and said, "When the cat's away the mice will play." Cece noticed that her mother's teeth were gritted and her fists clenched.

Cece knew she would be grounded. She wondered for how long. John had a short temper, and his punishments often involved a slap across the back plus being grounded. John cleared his throat and said calmly that the vase was very precious and that Cece could stay home for a month and not be allowed to read anything but school work. Cece knew that Amelia was upset and hurt over her loss. She dreaded the days ahead of looking out of the window with no books. At Christmas, Cece got Amelia a milk glass bud vase with money she had saved from selling pecans from the huge pecan tree in the back yard. John gave her two dollars as well, so Cece could get Ann and John something. Amelia liked the vase, or at least pretended she did. Cece felt less guilty, but she often remembered the broken vase.

28
RHYMING WORDS

Cece felt that Amelia didn't realize how much she liked poetry. Often at appropriate times, she would say one or more of the following rhymes that Cece learned and kept in her memory forever.

Amelia and Cece always had cold hands and especially cold feet. Whenever Cece complained about her cold feet, Amelia would say:

"Cold hands, warm heart,
Stinking feet, no sweetheart."

Cece didn't learn that cold feet and hands meant poor blood circulation until she was almost grown. She also didn't know if it was "sweetheart" or "sweet heart." She rather hoped it was the second one.

As Amelia taught Cece how to clean, she would often say:

"A man works from sun to sun,
a woman's work is never done."

Cece decided then and there that she would never get married, except to a rich man, so she could read instead of do housework and garden work.

The following are some of Amelia's wonderful rhymes. Where she got them, Cece never knew:

"A son is a son till he finds a wife,
A daughter's a daughter all of her life"
"Wear just a dab of perfume, no more;
Wear a lot, and you'll smell like a whore."

Cece looked up the last word the first time Amelia said it. She wondered if Amelia knew the meaning of the word. Here are some more:

"Beans, beans, the musical fruit,
The more you eat, the more you toot.
The more you toot, the better you feel,
So let's have beans for every meal."

"It's hard to find your lover,
When your heart is full of hope.
But it's harder still to find the towel,
When your eyes are full of soap."

Cece's favorite is the following. It taught her to really listen to friends, teachers, and even just acquaintances.

"The wise old owl in the old, old oak,
The more he heard, the less he spoke.
The less he spoke, the more he heard.
Why can't we be like that wise old bird?"

Amelia also loved the latest songs. Each week Cece helped iron the "rough" pieces, as Amelia called them. These were the sheets, pillow cases, socks, and all underwear. Cece hated ironing, but the one good part was that she could hear Amelia singing her favorite songs while she cooked. To this day, Cece remembers some of the tunes Amelia sang. She even remembers some of the words to several of the tunes. Amelia's favorite songs were "Alice Blue Gown," "Mary," "A Bicycle Built for Two," "Has Anybody Seen My Gal?" and "I Wonder What's Become of Sally."

Anyone who remembers those songs or even parts of those songs has a gift from the twenties.

29
A STITCH IN TIME...

Amelia finally relaxed her stronghold on economy after John kept adding to his wardrobe and even bought a piano that no one played. Cece had joined the Junior High Highlighters by practicing the clarinet by the hour in the back yard as far away from the house as she could get: Amelia's orders. The school provided the clarinet, which was a metal one, very heavy and hard to finger properly. If you wanted a wooden one, you had to buy it yourself.

One morning Amelia announced that it was 1943, the shop was doing well, and she had bought no new clothes for herself in years. She had heard from Miss Margie, her best friend, that old lady Johnson was the best seamstress in town. Amelia hit Belk Tyler's, the fabric store, like a northwester. She bought fabric, patterns, thread, buttons, and zippers. She had enough supplies to keep old lady Johnson busy for a year. Cece was as thrilled as Amelia, because Amelia hummed a lot and even smiled some every day. Cece still had a lot of hand-me-downs from her older cousin in Baltimore. In fact, Cece really wasn't into dresses and matching skirts and sweaters at all. What Cece wanted more than anything was a wooden clarinet and a fancy collar for Spot. The requests were denied by Amelia, who told her she would have old lady Johnson make her a dress. Cece could even pick out the fabric, but Amelia had to choose the pattern. After all, Cece was a teenager now, and you had to dress conservatively. Cece didn't want the dress and told Amelia so in a rather snippy tone.

Amelia walked out of the kitchen where she was cutting up a chicken for dinner. Cece picked up her metal clarinet, and she and Spot want to the back yard. Cece made sure she was closer to the house this time. She wanted Amelia to hear her.

30

DON'T SPEND IT ALL...

Cece was determined to get the wooden clarinet that the school did not provide. She was 13 and too young to get a work permit in North Carolina at that time; you had to be 14. But she knew John had connections all over the city because of the shop and the Elks Club. John knew Larry Midget, a city councilman and a fellow Elk's Club member, so he got Cece a work permit early.

The job was on Mr. W. S. Whaley's farm. Mr. Whaley was also an Elk, as well as the owner of a huge potato farm. Cece got a job on Mr. Whaley's farm grading potatoes with the fabulous salary of 75 cents an hour.

Work started at 6 a.m. It was very hot, hard, and dirty work. It was a five-days-a-week job, so Cece had weekends free. There was a big machine that rolled out a thing called a conveyer belt, which chugged along as a man at the end poured bushels of newly dug potatoes onto it. As the potatoes rolled by, the graders picked out any bruised or otherwise blemished potatoes and put them in a trough on each side of the belt. The potatoes rolled by fast, and the grader had to spot any less-than-perfect potatoes with great speed

Several young people from her school were working there, but none from her grade. Nevertheless, everyone was friendly, especially the young black girls from their school on the outskirts of town. This was the first time Cece had personal contact with black girls and she felt that both groups were pleasantly surprised as the girls talked about clothes, music, and boys. Then it got blazing hot and boring. All the other girls agreed that they had fun complaining about everything, even the amount of sweat they all produced. But the pay was good.

At the end of two weeks, when Cece got her first paycheck, Amelia took her to The First National Bank. Cece opened a checking account and felt very grown up. As they left the bank, Amelia said, "Don't spend it all in one place." Later that evening she said, "In fact you really shouldn't spend any of that money. You don't need anything."

Cece, who was going into seventh grade, did not spend it all in one place. First; she bought the wooden clarinet she wanted. Two pay checks later, she bought saddle shoes, the latest fashion of 1943. She bought the rest of the Nancy Drew books. Now she had the whole set published so far. A few weeks later, she bought Forever Amber, which a couple of her friends owned and kept rereading. Knitting was popular with the girls in school, so she bought an instruction book, yarn, and knitting needles, and started a sweater. Cece had never had so much fun in her life. She even managed to save a few dollars in her bank account before school started that fall. Every time she brought home a package, Amelia asked her how much money she was saving. Cece diverted Amelia's attention by showing Amelia the new purchase. In due course, Spot also sported a new bright red collar. Indeed Cece had not spent it all in one place.

31

THINGS DON'T SPROUT LEGS

Cece knew she was an unorganized person, for Amelia had told her so many times. It was true that Cece was always looking for something: her clarinet, her sweater, or mostly a book. She would take a homework or library book wherever she went to read or study, then, of course, she would put it down. Usually she forgot where she left it and the hunt would begin later.

One day Cece misplaced a library book that was due the very next day. First, she retraced her steps to the last places where she had been. No luck. Then she carefully checked each room, including on, over, and under each piece of furniture. No luck. Amelia had often told Cece that "things didn't sprout legs and walk out of the house," so Cece was reluctant to ask Amelia to join the search. In desperation, Cece checked each closet. She searched each of the drawers in her bedroom dresser. Would Amelia hide the book to teach her to be more careful? Cece didn't think so. Nevertheless, she went through the drawers in Amelia and John's bedroom. Cece was completely frustrated by then. She felt flushed, angry at everything. Her footsteps became heavy. She was practically stomping around the house.

The noise, of course, drew Amelia to the scene. Amelia automatically knew Cece was looking for something. After Cece told her that the fine for a late library book was ten cents a day, Amelia immediately joined the search.

Finally, Cece remembered that she had been out in the backyard under the mulberry tree. Amelia and Cece bolted out the door, down the steps, and to the far back of the yard. There sat *A Tale of Two Cities*. Amelia looked at Cece wide-eyed, saying, "If your arse weren't bolted on you would misplace it." Cece never forgot that expression, because at the time it seemed very true.

32
THE BEST PART OF A CHICKEN...

Chicken was the standard Sunday dinner at Cece's home. Any meat was a Sunday special. Amelia knew many ways to concoct delicious Sunday fare. She made fried chicken, baked chicken, chicken gumbo, or chicken and dumplings. Sunday chicken lasted through Tuesday in the form of salad or soup. Appropriately, John always got the breast. Cece favored a leg, known as the drumstick. Amelia swore the best part of the chicken went over the fence last. John and Cece never denied Amelia her favorite part. Cece later found out that this part of the chicken was called "the Pope's nose" in her best friend's home.

33

SEX EDUCATION... AMELIA-STYLE

When Cece hit dating age, she would date a boy just to test him out. She had no exact criteria for liking a boy, but she was pretty fussy. Amelia, on the other hand, had firmly established standards she kept imparting to Cece.

One summer Cece started dating Joe, a boy from Weeksville, a village several miles away from E. City. Cece liked him because he was older than she, four years to be exact. When Amelia realized this, she was adamantly against the relationship. But Cece was now 17 and asserted her right to date whomever she pleased.

Amelia never overtly voiced her personal dislike for Joe, but Cece knew Amelia's opinion about men from her "words of wisdom.". Amelia had told Cece nothing about "the birds and the bees," as Cece's best friend called it. Cece learned a lot in health class, which she had during all four years of high school. But Amelia's sayings went as follows:

"Beware of flatterers."

"Handsome is as handsome does."

"Boys are wolves in sheep's clothing."

"What you date at 17, you won't look at at 20."

"Never put the cart before the horse." (This one took a while to figure out.)

"Your reputation is everything."

"Don't let a boy pull the wool over your eyes."

"Virtue is well rewarded."

"He's nothing to write home about. "And the single question Amelia ALWAYS asked:

"What does his daddy do?" (Cece seldom knew the answer to this.)

Cece had some patience for Amelia's words of "wisdom" about boys, but she liked boys and dating and never asked what any of her boyfriends' fathers did. Cece really liked the way Amelia would give her a new "opinion" about boys as she was drying dishes or getting dressed for a date. They actually helped keep Cece on the alert for wandering hands, and Cece realized that Amelia's warning words flashed through her mind whenever a boy tried something. Cece promptly enforced Amelia's convictions, which were now a part of her own sense of what was right.

34
HOME MEDICINE

Cece was a sickly kid but doctor visits cost money and were beyond the budget. Cece's first and only visit to a doctor was at 18 when she had to have a physical examination to enter college. No matter what Cece caught, Amelia would diagnosis it and give remedy.

Where Amelia learned her healing techniques, Cece never knew. but Cece learned them all. She also attained adulthood.

Diagnosis:
First she felt your forehead. Then said: "You are green around the gills".

Remedies:
Ear ache: Hot wet rag on aching ear.
Headache: Sleep
Cough:
> - 1 cup of hot tea
> - 1 tablespoon honey
> - a squeeze of lemon juice

Take when needed. Take before going to sleep.

Fever or Cold: "Starve a fever", feed a cold.
Cuts, scrapes, bruises: Wrap ice in towel, place on wound.
Anything unidentified: If ice or cold water won't work, it's serious.
Measles, mumps, everything else: "It will get well before you get married".

35

MIND YOUR MANNERS

Perhaps it was just a southern thing Amelia picked up as a child because she had no mother as a role model. Maybe it was the aunt who raised her and her three sisters who set the right example. Whatever it was, Amelia dictated her absorbed behaviors to her daughters. Certainly these manners are still appropriate.

"Always put a napkin in your lap before eating". (We often used a dish towel when lacking napkins)

"Don't talk with your mouth full".

"Never interrupt an adult". (Today's younger generation could use this one.)

"Put your left hand in your lap while eating". (Right hand is lapped if left handed)

"Chew with your mouth CLOSED".

"Never, never pick your nose in public".

"Never, never spit, even if it's at an inanimate object".

"Always write a thank you note for a gift you receive".

"Always cover your mouth/nose when you cough or sneeze".

"Always wear good underpants when going out in case you end up in the hospital".

"Never burp out loud".

"Never fart in public."

"Never fart at the table".

36

NEW GUIDANCE

Cece loved English class, because they had lots of reading assignments. In fifth grade, Cece had the first teacher who stressed punctuation. Mrs. Flood wore thick glasses, along with mainly brown or black outfits of skirt, sweater, and white blouse. She had taught a long time, but was still cheerful each day and understanding about people in the band who often had to miss a class. Cece was grateful, because she loved being in the band, especially the part about marching on the football field during half-time at football games, whether in Elizabeth City or in Edenton and in schools even farther away than Edenton.

One day in April, Mrs. Flood read several poems by Robert Frost and Emily Dickinson. Cece was transfixed. She especially loved Frost's "Mending Walls." She went to the library at the end of the school day and took out a poetry anthology.

Mrs. Flood had given the class three days to write a poem at least eight lines long. Cece spent hours writing that poem. It was, of course, about spring, and Mrs. Flood read it aloud to the class. Cece's heart beat fast, and she held her head down because her face was red. From then on Cece kept a notebook for her poems.

Her senior year in 1948, Cece had Miss Nancy Marker for English. She was young with red hair that curled just right at the ends. She was the same height as Cece, which meant she was short, just over five feet. She had a great smile and a wonderful way of making "Romeo and Juliet" fun by assigning parts to several students from one scene in the play. Then she gave them a few days to read their parts so each person would understand the meaning of Shakespeare's words. Then each group acted out their roles. After finishing the play, they had a "feast" of pizza.

One day, Miss Marker had Cece and three other students return to her classroom, after school to take the Scholastic Aptitude Test. Cece thought the math was hard, but the rest was easy. Several days later Miss Marker called Cece aside and asked her if she had thought about going to college. Cece hadn't. Miss Marker suggested that Cece talk to her parents about it. Cece nodded, wondering what college was like. She knew that her friends Nancy, Peggy, and Dorothy were going to college, because they had told everyone. But their parents were rich and they lived in big houses. Cece felt a little afraid to mention it to Amelia, but she knew she had to, because college appealed to her.

A few nights later, as Cece dried the dishes, she told Amelia that she wanted to go to college and Miss Marker had told her she had the ability to do well there. Amelia kept on washing the dishes, as if she hadn't heard Cece. When she finished the dishes, she took the dish cloth from Cece and said, "College costs a lot of money. Don't hold your breath."

Every time Cece mentioned what she would like to do after graduating just a few months later, Amelia would give Cece a few words of discouragement. Some of these were:

"What kind of a job can you get after college"?

"Money doesn't grow on trees."

"Go tell it on the mountain."

"You can't squeeze blood from a turnip."

"If wishes were horses, we would all ride."

"Don't count your chickens before they hatch."

"Don't hold your breath." (this she said most frequently.)

Cece didn't hold her breath. With Miss Marker's help, she applied to Women's College in Greensboro, was accepted, and got a scholarship in return for working 20 hours a week in the college dining hall, as well as the library.

Elizabeth City
High School Faculty
1948

37

SHADES OF SHAKESPEARE

Because of Miss Marker, Cece looked forward to taking Shakespeare in her sophomore year in college. She didn't realize until then that many of the adages that Amelia told her were what Shakespeare had said in a more poetic way. The following are quotes from Shakespeare, followed by Amelia's sayings that show the wisdom she gave to Cece:

Willie: "Stand not by the order of your going." – "*Macbeth*"
Amelia:" Don't let the door hit you in the arsch when you leave".

Willie: "Sleep dwell upon thine eyes, peace on thy breast."
    – "*Romeo and Juliet*"
Amelia: "Good night, sleep tight,
    don't let the bedbugs bite."

Willie: "Good name in man and woman, dear my lord,
    Is the immediate jewel of their soul." – "*Othello*"
Amelia: "Your reputation is everything."

Willie: "The jewel that we find, we stoop and take it,
    Because we see it; but what we do not see
    We tread upon and never think of it." – "*Measure for Measure*"
Amelia: "You never miss what you don't know."

Willie: "The labor we delight in physics pain." –"*Macbeth*"
Amelia:" Be sure to like what you do or you'll be miserable."

Willie: "But since all is well, keep it so,
    Wake not a sleeping wolf." – "*Henry IV*"
Amelia: "Let sleeping dogs lie."

Willie: "All that glistens is not gold;
    Often have you heard that told." – "*The Merchant of Venice*"
Amelia: "You can't judge a book by its cover."

Willie: "Things without all remedy
    Should be without regard:
    What's done is done." – "*Macbeth*"
Amelia: "Don't cry over spilt milk"
        and
    "That's water over the dam."

Willie: "Trust not thy physician." – "*Timon of Athens*"
Amelia: "Always get a second opinion."

Willie: "Better three hours too soon than one minute too late."
    – "*The Merry Wives of Windsor*"
Amelia: "The early bird gets the worm." (Something she
    never practiced.)

Willie: "Misery acquaints a man with strange bedfellows."
    – "*The Tempest*"
Amelia: "Misery loves company.

38

AT THE WAKE

I touch her hand.
It is cold wax,
every raised vein the same,
fingers curved slightly
the way they always rested
on her lap,
but so cold, so still.

I touch
to verify the real
to feel death,
though in her blue dress with white roses
she looks as if she is dozing
before going
out to dinner.

This is man's ritual
for closure,
for making sure,
so I can let go,
and the loss
becomes more true
than all her life.

39

A FEW WORDS FROM JOHN

John, being basically shy, became even less of a communicator as time went on due to his lack of education. But John was a happy man in his own way and enjoyed being around people. He did have a short fuse when things didn't go his way, so Cece had a love/fear feeling about him. But she cherished every word he said to her, probably because he said so few.

Here are the words of "wisdom" John imparted to Cece, though the specific occasions have been forgotten:

"Do as I say, not as I do."

"Another day, another dollar."

"As long as you put your feet under my table, you will do as I say."

(This would be elicited by any item of food Cece didn't want to eat or any curfew Cece felt was unfair.)

"You can't take it with you."

"Look it up." (John's response to almost anything Cece asked him about any school subject)

"Go ask your mother." (concerning anything that involved asking permission)

"I'm going to see a man about a dog." (anytime Cece asked him where he was going)

"Just because there's snow on the roof doesn't mean there's no fire in the cellar." (It took Cece a long time to figure this one out.)

40
THE GIFT

How many times will my husband, sons, daughter
tell me, tell me, tell me
to stop biting my fingernails,
the substitute for cigarettes
I gave up at my father's request
as he gasped the name of my mother
who was a statue sitting outside
at the end of the hall
and would not move into
the five minutes given us each hour.
He said nothing for a while,
his cheeks sunbursts on the winter of his face,
the room; a cockpit of clicks, blips, bleeps, drips
from instruments and tubes that
told me nothing.
Suddenly he mouthed my name,
rasped his request,
not moving as he gave me his best gift.
All ten of these nails will grow again,
and then I must, absolutely must
nibble, twist, pull,
rip the edges up
to the quicks of the fingers
that did not reach for his hand.

41

A FEW WORDS FROM OTHERS

Through the years, Cece gleaned some other sayings that she treasured. Here are a few:

"You are what you are."– *Cathy Taylor*

"What you see is what you see."– *Frank Stella*

"Don't be afraid to see what you see,"– *Ronald Reagan*

"Nothing comes from nothing."– *Shakespeare, "King Lear"*

"The day we left felt like the day we got there."– *Samantha Saloom*; age 8, about her vacation

"Why do we say inside out? Why don't we say outside in?"
– *Alex Gardner*, age 5, about his ski hat

"Frustration causes accidents. Please allow overtaking."
– *British road sign*

"God couldn't be everywhere, so He made mothers."
– *Jewish proverb*

"A work of art is a hopeful thing." – *Richard Russo*

"The only reason for time is so that everything doesn't happen at once." – *Albert Einstein*

"Creativity is intelligence having fun." – *Albert Einstein*

"I have always loved solitude, a trait that tends to increase with age."
– *Albert Einstein*

"A foolish faith in authority is the worst enemy of truth"
– *Albert Einstein*

"Don't spend your money before you have it" – *Thomas Jefferson*

"How much pain have cost us the evils which have never happened."
–*Thomas Jefferson*

"I have my principles; if you don't like them, I have others."– *Groucho Marx*

"If you don't work, you don't eat." – *Captain John Smith,*
Jamestown, VA, 1608

"It's easier to ask forgiveness than permission." – *John Bindas,
school principal*

"Cutting your own firewood warms you twice." – *New England saying*

"To teach is to learn." – *Japanese proverb*

"The oxen are slow, but the earth is patient."
– *"High Road to China"*, film

"I gave up wine once. Worst day of my life" – *Grimm*

"Whatever you do, do it with all your might,
things done in half are never done right." – *Margie Peterson*

"If you are not early you're late" – *Mildred Taylor*

Many of the old clichés have disappeared from our everyday conversations. They are considered to be antiques, trite and useless. But to Cece they were the roots on which her outlook on life flourished. Cece hopes that these adages that she has passed on through this book inspire us to rethink their value.

Cece saved Amelia's favorite and most used adage for last. It should help us all, every one:

"A penny saved is not enough." – *Amelia Pearson*

42

TRIBUTES

The following poems are for Cece's parents:

<u>JULY 20, 1969</u>

Daddy stands in the hall,
curls his index finger for me to come there.
His chalk legs bend at the knees, tremble.
I speed my steps.
He glances around, sees no one,
whispers a question.

I tell him of the reflecting rock
thick with dust, little gravity,
windless and waterless,
with blistering days, frigid nights
where a man stands
planting a stiff flag.

My father, orphaned at eight,
never finished third grade.
He learned roofing, painting, plumbing by twelve,
found his profession at fourteen …
Straightening dented metal
on automobiles.

This man
three weeks before death
wanted to know gravity,
motion,
wanted to know
the moon.

Daddy's eyes shine as I stop talking.
He nods,
shuffles back into his bedroom.
His TV blares, crackles. I watch
as he watches once more
a rigid flag standing.

MY MOTHER'S MYTHS

Orange eyes stare from the plate,
carrots will make my broom-straw hair curly,
taste of rust down my throat in lumps,
the mirror never lies,
but hope doesn't die until I am nine.

Head down, eyes bolted to feet,
I watch each step like an eagle.
Don't slow down, never stumble,
keep pace exactly even for
stepping on a crack in the sidewalk breaks your mother's back.
She meets me at the door,
eyes squint, hands on hips,
voile dress clings like tattoos,
a tigress eyeing her wayward prey.
Shame prods me to eat foods.
I picture thousands of Chinese children,
fingers of their ribs clawing empty bellies.
One day in school I spin the globe
until I find China,
wonder how long it would take
my class to dig a hole through the earth,
drop our extra food to these children.

If I cross my eyes, they will freeze that way forever,
a tooth turns into a dime under my pillow,
rabbits lay eggs, December tapping on windows,
the Boogie Man judges every move.
These tenets dictate my behavior like oracles.

I did not give these myths to my children,
but I hold them like shells shaped by the ocean
or stones smoothed by wind and rain

COLOPHON

Text for this book was set in Adobe Garamond.
Printed and bound by 360 Digital Books of Livonia, Michigan.